Copyright © 2020 The Coloring Cafe
All rights reserved.
No part of this book may be reproduced or transmitted in any form
or by any means, electronic or mechanical, including photocopying,
recording or by any information storage and retrieval system,
without permission in writing from the publisher.

ISBN-13: 978-1-56383-590-2
Item #2507

Printed in the USA   www.cqbookstore.com

Distributed By: gifts@cqbookstore.com

 CQ Products

 CQ Products

 @cqproducts

 @cqproducts

PO Box 850
Waverly, IA 50677

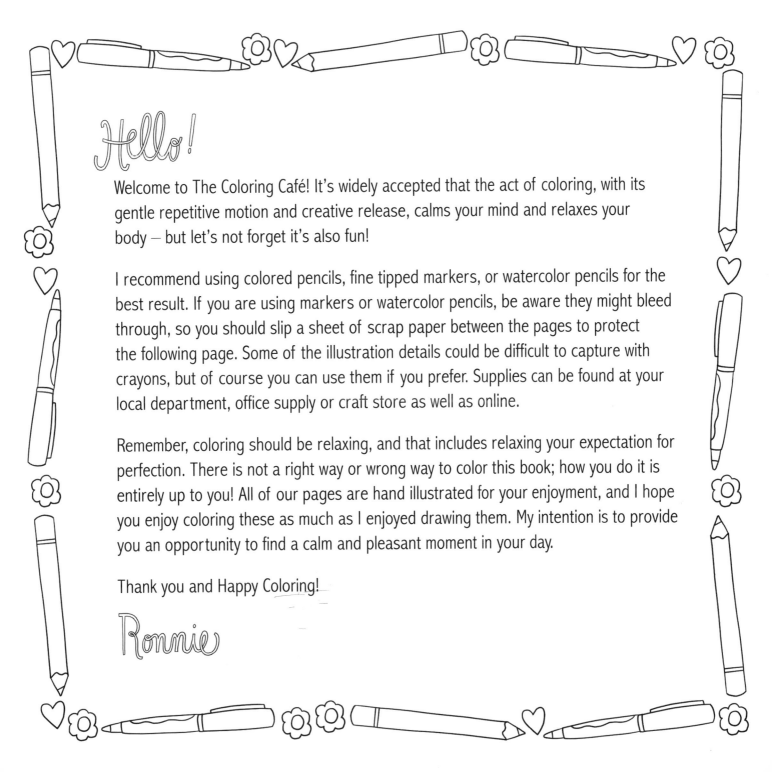

Hello!

Welcome to The Coloring Café! It's widely accepted that the act of coloring, with its gentle repetitive motion and creative release, calms your mind and relaxes your body — but let's not forget it's also fun!

I recommend using colored pencils, fine tipped markers, or watercolor pencils for the best result. If you are using markers or watercolor pencils, be aware they might bleed through, so you should slip a sheet of scrap paper between the pages to protect the following page. Some of the illustration details could be difficult to capture with crayons, but of course you can use them if you prefer. Supplies can be found at your local department, office supply or craft store as well as online.

Remember, coloring should be relaxing, and that includes relaxing your expectation for perfection. There is not a right way or wrong way to color this book; how you do it is entirely up to you! All of our pages are hand illustrated for your enjoyment, and I hope you enjoy coloring these as much as I enjoyed drawing them. My intention is to provide you an opportunity to find a calm and pleasant moment in your day.

Thank you and Happy Coloring!

Ronnie

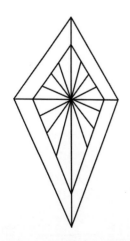

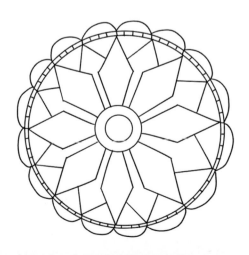

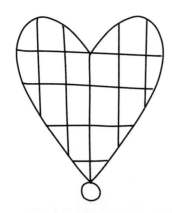

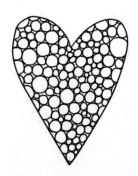

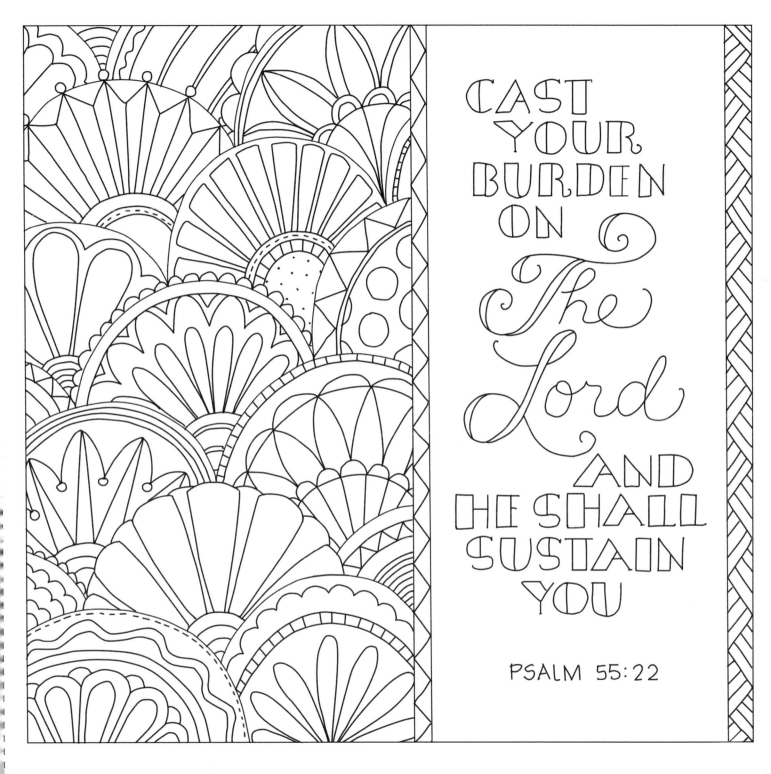

About the Artist

Ronnie Walter has known since she could first hold a crayon what she wanted to do with her life, and that little girl who could draw really well grew up to be a professional artist and author. Her illustrations have been featured on hundreds of products such as stationery and greeting cards, figurines, home and garden products, fabric and much more. She is especially proud of her work creating the Coloring Café® series of coloring books, and of the joy they have brought to thousands of her "Coloristas."

Ronnie lives in paradise with her husband Jim and their colorful Catahoula hound, Larry.

www.thecoloringcafe.com

coloringcafe@gmail.com

 Coloring Café

 The Coloring Café

 @thecoloringcafe

 @thecoloringcafe

Complete your collection...

with all the coloring products for grown-up girls by The Coloring Café.

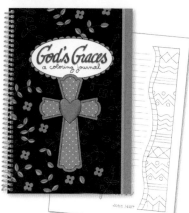   

www.cqbookstore.com